STEP INTO SCIENCE

OVER THE RAINBOW!

The Science of Color and Light

BARBARA TAYLOR

Random House 🏠 New York

COLOR AND LIGHT

In this book, you will discover how we see colors, how we use colors for painting and printing, and how light is made up of all the colors of the rainbow.

The book is divided into eight different subjects. Watch for the big headings with a circle at each end—like the one at the top of this page. These headings tell you where a new subject starts.

Pages 4–5

How Many Colors?

Collecting and sorting colors.

Pages 10–13

Painting Colors

Mixing colors; brushes and textures.

Pages 6–9

Seeing Colors

Animal eyesight; human eyesight; color blindness; safety colors.

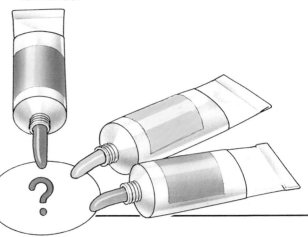

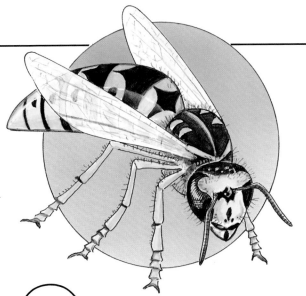

HOW MANY COLORS?

Make a collection of different colored objects like the ones along the edges of these two pages. Look for some natural materials as well as artificial ones. Sort your collection into sets, such as happy and sad colors or summer and winter colors. How many different shades of the same color can you find?

Another way of sorting your collection would be to put all the things made from the same material (such as paper, plastic, or cloth) together.

▶ How many different colors can you find in the picture? What is your favorite color?

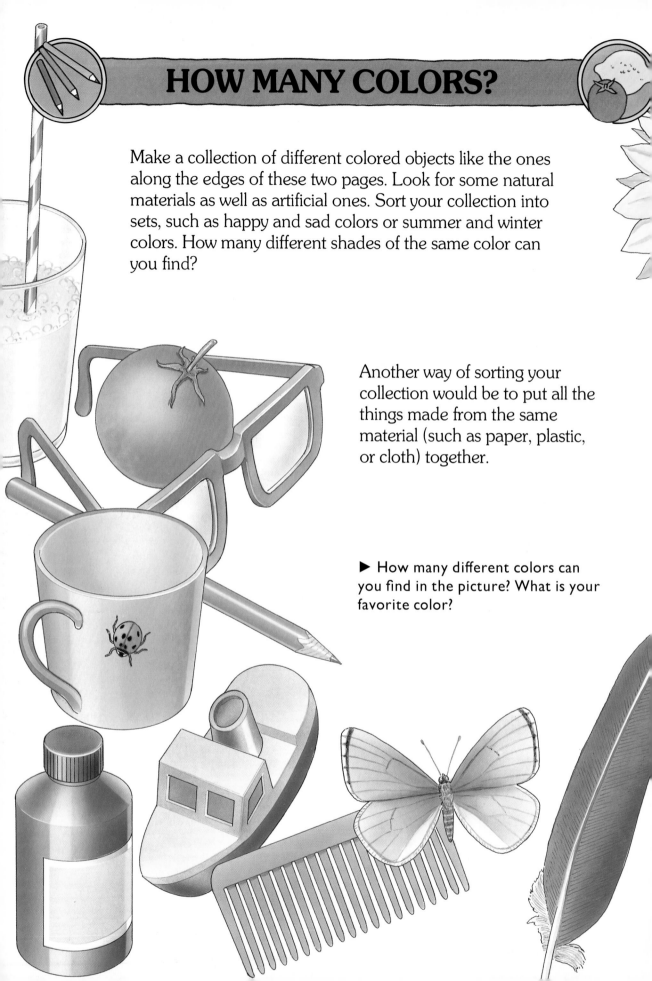

SEEING COLORS

We see things because light bounces off objects into our eyes. This "bouncing off" effect is called reflection. The light from the sun or an electric light bulb looks white, but it is really made up of all the colors of the rainbow. (See pages 24–27.) The colors we see depend on the colors that are reflected off objects into our eyes. For instance, a tomato looks red because it reflects red light and absorbs the other colors.

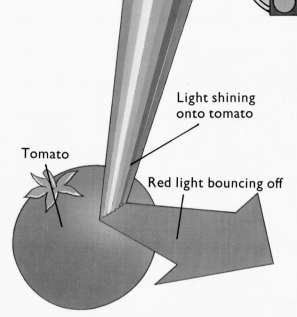

Tomato

Light shining onto tomato

Red light bouncing off

If an object absorbs all the rainbow colors in light, no light is reflected and we see black. If an object reflects all the colors, we see white.

Animal Eyesight

Did you know that many animals, such as cats, dogs, horses, and cows, cannot see the colors we see? Their world is full of shades of black and white and gray. Apes and monkeys, however, seem to be able to see the same colors that we can, and some animals, especially birds, may have better color vision than we do. Animals that are brightly colored can nearly always see colors.

Your view

Dog's view

Human Eyesight

We see colors because of special cells that make up part of the lining of the eyeball. These cells are cone-shaped, so they are called cones. In each eye, there are about 7 million cones. One type of cone responds to red light, a second type responds to green light, and a third type responds to blue light. The cones send messages to the brain, and by joining together the messages it receives, the brain tells us what colors we are seeing.

This test shows you more about how you see colors. Draw a red shape on a piece of white paper. Stare hard at your drawing for a minute. Then stare at a blank piece of white paper. What color do you see now? Repeat the test with a blue object.

What happens

The cones that respond to red light quickly get tired and stop working for a while. When you stare at the white paper, only the green and blue cones are working. So you see a green-blue picture. This color is called cyan. With the blue object, only the red and green cones are working, so you see yellow.

Color Blindness

Some people are color blind, which means they cannot tell the difference between certain colors. Very few people are truly color blind, seeing only black, white, and gray.

7

Color Messages

Which colors stand out best from a distance? Stick paper of one color onto different backgrounds, or stick different colors onto the same background.

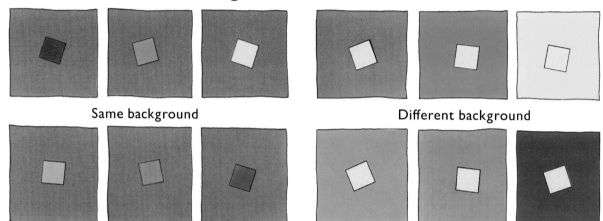

Same background   Different background

Ask a friend to hold up the different combinations at a distance. Which combination of colors stands out best? Are some colors more affected by the background color than others? Which colors would you use for signs in a desert, a snowy mountain, or a forest?

Remembering Colors

Are some colors easier to remember than others? Look at this picture for a minute. Then shut the book. How many of the objects can you remember? Can you remember the color of each object? You could record your results and compare them with those of your friends.

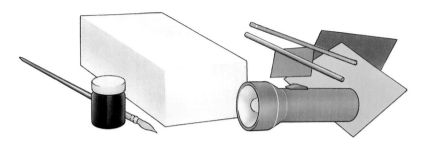

Safety Colors

At night or in a dark room, it is hard to see colors. This is because the cones in your eyes need a lot of light to work properly. But sometimes colors need to stand out in the dark, so they can be seen at night, in the dim light of tunnels or movie theaters, or by people with poor eyesight. Which colors show up well in dim light?

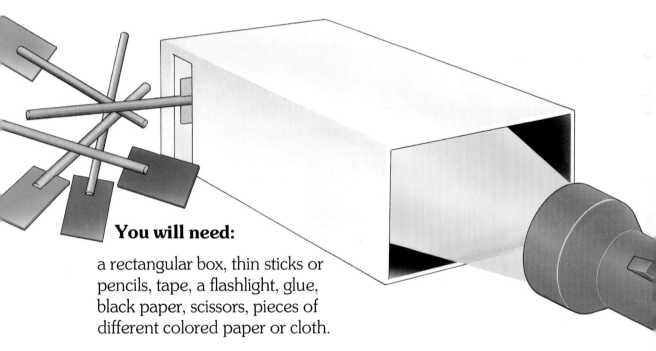

You will need:

a rectangular box, thin sticks or pencils, tape, a flashlight, glue, black paper, scissors, pieces of different colored paper or cloth.

1. With an adult's help, cut off one end of the box. Near the other end of the box, cut a slit in one side.
2. Cover the inside of the box with black paper.
3. Cut small pieces of the paper or cloth.
4. Stick each piece of paper or cloth in turn onto the stick or pencil and poke it through the slit in the box.
5. Shine a flashlight into the open end of the box. Which colors show up best in the dim light?

Paints used to be made from natural pigments, which are colored powders formed by grinding up materials such as soil, rocks, plants, shellfish, or even dead insects. All these things have a natural color. Nowadays, chemists use both natural and artificial pigments to produce paints.

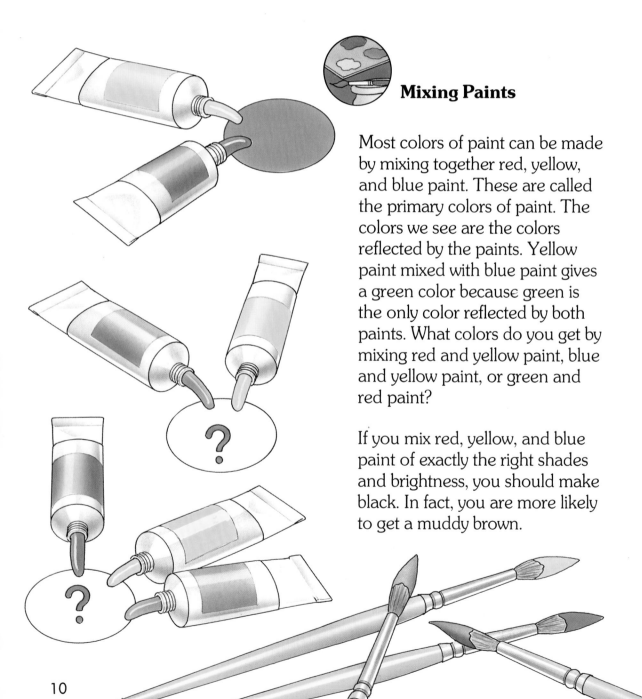

Mixing Paints

Most colors of paint can be made by mixing together red, yellow, and blue paint. These are called the primary colors of paint. The colors we see are the colors reflected by the paints. Yellow paint mixed with blue paint gives a green color because green is the only color reflected by both paints. What colors do you get by mixing red and yellow paint, blue and yellow paint, or green and red paint?

If you mix red, yellow, and blue paint of exactly the right shades and brightness, you should make black. In fact, you are more likely to get a muddy brown.

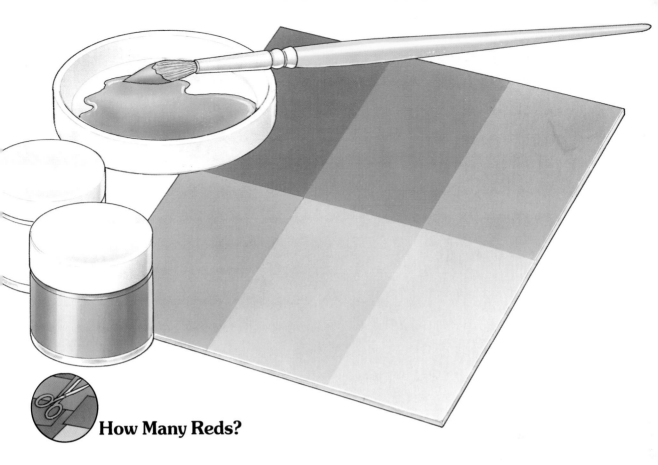

How Many Reds?

Have you ever looked at the paint charts in hardware stores? You can buy lots of different shades of one color, and it is often hard to choose the right one for your room.

See if you can mix up six shades of one color, such as red. Divide a piece of paper into six equal-sized strips. Put bright red paint in the first strip and then keep adding white paint, a little at a time, to make lighter reds. When the paint is dry, write a number on the back of each strip. Make one the deepest color and six the palest color. Then cut up all the squares and mix them up. Can you sort them back into the right order?

Cork

Feather

Shapes and Textures

Sponge

Paintbrushes are good at soaking up paint. What other materials can you use to paint with? Make a collection of things such as crumpled paper, cork, a sponge, and feathers. How good are fruits and vegetables at soaking up paint? Mix some paint in a saucer and dip each object into the paint in turn. Press the objects firmly onto some paper. How many different shapes and textures can you make? You could sign your paintings with a hand print.

Apple

You can use apples to make interesting shapes. With an adult's help, cut an apple in half and brush lots of paint over the cut surface. Press it down firmly onto some plain paper. If you cut the apple across the middle, you can make star shapes. What shapes do you make if you cut the apple in half from top to bottom?

Fingers

◀ Face and body painting changes the way we look. These people from Papua New Guinea have painted their faces for a celebration.

Hand

Potato Print

Ask an adult to help you carve a shape in the cut surface of a potato. The shape has to stand out from the surface. Paint the shape and press it down onto the paper.

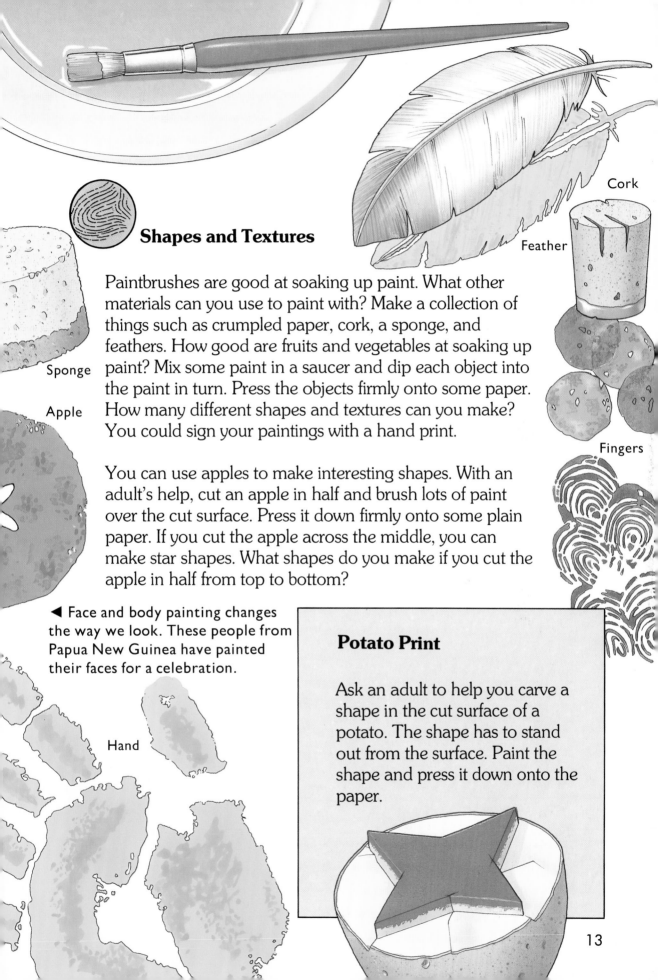

13

MAKING COLORS

As well as paints, there are several other coloring materials, such as wax crayons, colored pencils, chalk, charcoal, ink, and felt pens. Draw an outline shape several times and color each one with a different coloring material. How do they look different? Which coloring material is easiest to use? Which do you like best? What happens if you use the coloring materials on a wet surface? Do they mix with water?

▼ Stone Age artists painted the walls of these caves 12,000–30,000 years ago. They mixed their colors from natural pigments in the soil, rocks, or minerals. They ground the pigments into a smooth paste with pestles and mortars and then blended the colors on stone palettes. The colors were probably mixed with animal fat to make them waterproof. The artists used brushes made of animal hair, chewed twigs, and pads of moss and fur. All their paintings were done using only the flickering light from small lamps that burned animal fat.

Making Yellow Dye

You will need:
2 ounces of alum, 1 tablespoon of cream of tartar, 1 ounce of onion skins, white cloth, a sieve, 2 large saucepans, a jar.

You can use the colored juices from plants to dye cloth or wool. Some dyes do not give permanent colors unless another chemical is added. These chemicals are called mordants. They "fix" the color by making it bite into the cloth so the colors last. In the past, tree bark and wood ash have been used as mordants. Nowadays, you can buy artificial mordants from the pharmacist.

Ask an adult to help you with this project.

1. Mix the alum and cream of tartar with 17 fluid ounces of warm water in the jar. Add to a large pan of cold water.
2. Put the cloth in the pan and heat it gradually. Stir until it boils.
3. Simmer gently for about an hour, then let it cool down.
4. Take out the cloth and put it in a plastic bag. Discard the liquid.
5. Boil the onion skins in a deep pan full of water, then simmer for an hour.
6. Strain the liquid through a sieve to get rid of the skins.

Cream of tartar

Alum

7. Put your damp cloth into the pan with the onion liquid and bring to a boil again. Simmer gently for one hour.
8. Switch off the heat and let the pan cool.
9. Take the cloth out of the pan and rinse it thoroughly.
10. Let the cloth dry.

Other Colors from Plants

Now make dyes from other plants, such as spinach, tea leaves, red cabbage, pine cones, and blackberries. You can also dye yarn instead of cloth.

Colored Patterns

There are several different ways of making colored patterns in cloth. In tie-dyeing, part of the cloth is tied up to stop the dye from reaching that part of the cloth. When the tie is removed, white patterns are left in the colored material. If you do this yourself, you can knot the cloth or use string or rubber bands to tie it. You can also fold the cloth before you tie it, or put objects such as pebbles, buttons, and seeds in the cloth to create a different pattern.

You can also make different colors by dyeing the same piece of material in several colors, one after another.

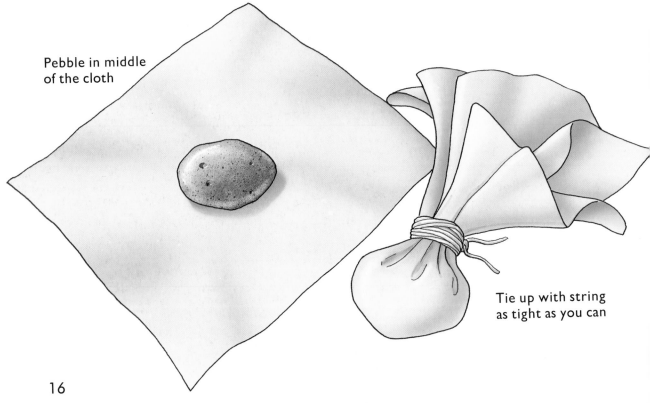

Pebble in middle
of the cloth

Tie up with string
as tight as you can

16

▲ Cloth that has been tie-dyed can be used to make all sorts of clothing.

◀ Batik dyeing involves dropping hot, melted wax onto the cloth. The waxed areas do not take up the dye, and when the wax is washed off, it leaves beautiful patterns in the cloth. You can see how this works by drawing a picture with a wax crayon or an unlit candle and then painting over it.

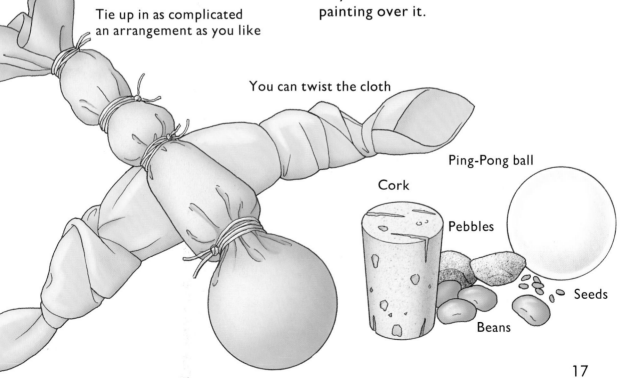

Tie up in as complicated an arrangement as you like

You can twist the cloth

Cork

Ping-Pong ball

Pebbles

Seeds

Beans

Kitchen Chemicals

You can use a solution of colored dye to find out if chemicals found in the kitchen are acids or alkalis. Acids and alkalis are chemical opposites. They behave differently when they are mixed with other chemicals. A dye that changes color when it is mixed with acids or alkalis is called an indicator. You can make an indicator from red cabbage.

1. With an adult's help, chop up some red cabbage leaves and put them in a bowl.
2. Add a little sand and mash the leaves with the back of an old spoon. The sand helps to break up the cabbage leaves so the dye can get out.
3. Ask an adult to add some very hot water to the bowl. Let the cabbage soak until cool.
4. Pour the liquid through a sieve

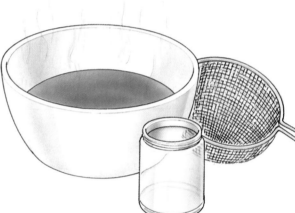

to get rid of the cabbage leaves. You will be left with a colored indicator solution. Put this into a bottle or jar with a lid.
5. In saucers or jars, mix small amounts of the indicator solution with some of the different chemicals in the kitchen. Good things to try are lemon juice, baking powder, vinegar, laundry detergent, and soapy water.

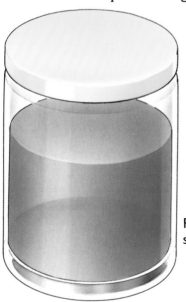

Put dye in screw top jar

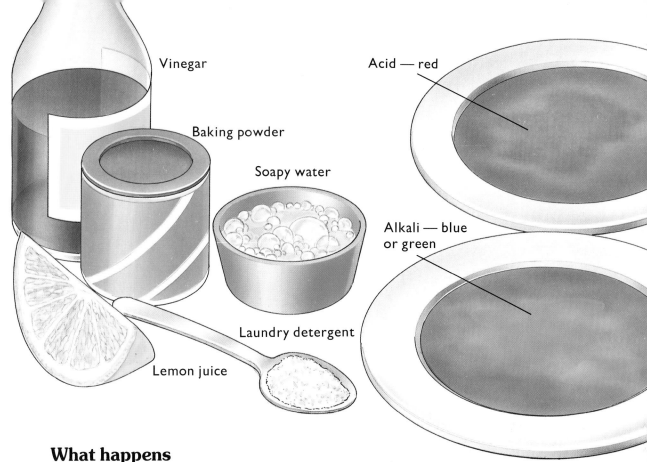

Vinegar

Baking powder

Soapy water

Laundry detergent

Lemon juice

Acid — red

Alkali — blue or green

What happens

If acidic chemicals are mixed with the indicator solution, it will turn red or orange. If the chemicals are alkaline, the solution will turn blue or green. How many acids and alkalis can you find?

Did You Know?

The poison in a bee sting is an acid, and the poison in a wasp sting is an alkali.

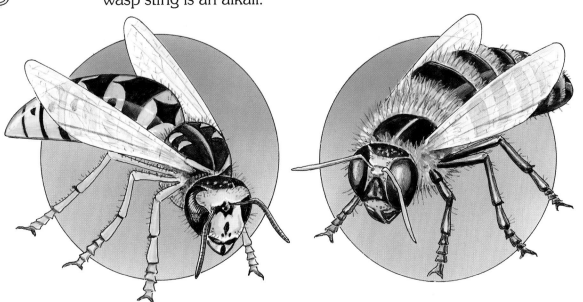

Color Pictures

Many of the pigments we use appear to be one color but are really made up of mixtures of colors. You can separate these colors using a technique called chromatography—the word means "color pictures."

You will need:
felt-tip pens (especially dark colors, such as brown and black), a pencil, tape, a jar of water, blotting paper, scissors, cotton balls.

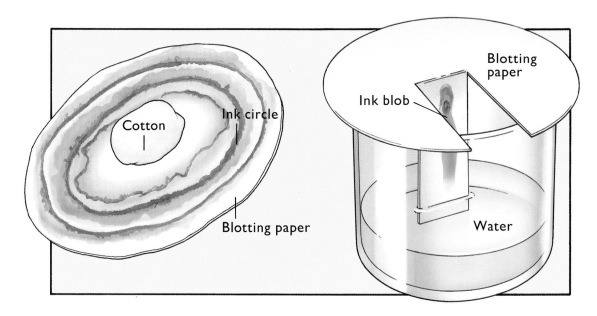

1. With an adult's help, cut up several small circles of blotting paper.
2. Draw a ring of color in the middle of some of the circles.
3. Soak balls of cotton in some water and put them in the center of the colored rings. Watch the colors spread out.
4. Cut a strip in some of the circles to match the picture.
5. Put a small dot of color on the bottom of the strip near the fold.
6. Put some water in the jar and let the strip hang down so it just touches the water. Before you put each strip in the water, see if you can guess which colors you will see.
7. Now try other sources, such as food coloring, inks, and candy.

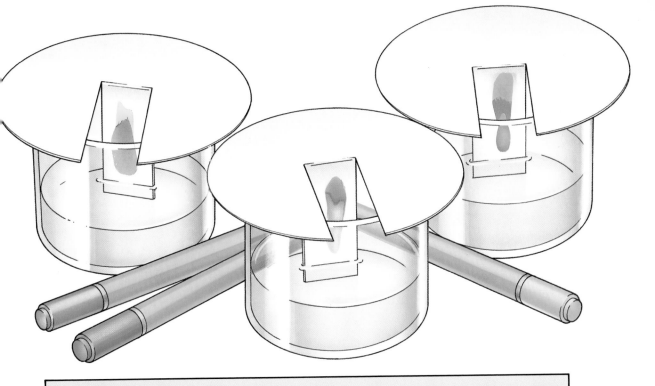

What happens

As the water spreads through the blotting paper, it carries the color with it. If the pens are made up of several different pigments, you will see bands of different colors. Some pigments contain bigger, heavier particles than others, so the pigments spread out at different speeds. Smaller, lighter particles move faster and farther, leaving the bigger ones behind.

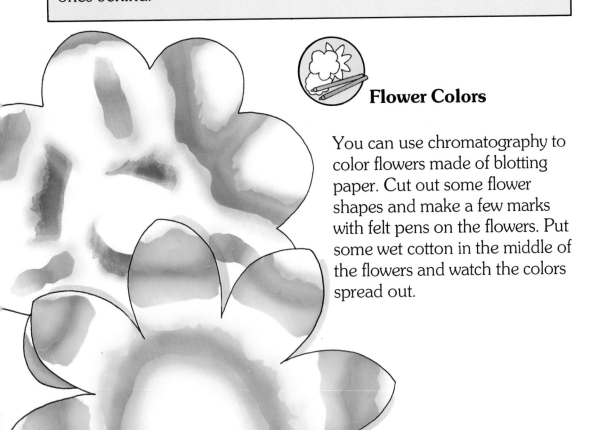

Flower Colors

You can use chromatography to color flowers made of blotting paper. Cut out some flower shapes and make a few marks with felt pens on the flowers. Put some wet cotton in the middle of the flowers and watch the colors spread out.

Lots of Dots

Use a magnifying glass to look closely at the pictures in a newspaper. You will see that each one is made up of lots of black dots. The dots are largest in the dark areas and very small in the pale areas. The pale areas look gray, even though only black ink is used.

Book Colors

The color pictures in a book are also made up of lots of dots. The original picture is broken down into four colors—the primary pigments red, blue, and yellow, plus black. The black helps to add fine detail and make some areas darker.

Each color is printed as tiny dots. Because the dots are so small, our eyes can't see them—unless we use a magnifying glass. So we see areas of flat color, which look like the original colors of the picture. If the dots are not printed in exactly the right place, the picture looks fuzzy.

Blue is a blue-green color called cyan   Red is a pink-re color called ma,

Dotty Television

The colors of a television picture are also made up of a pattern of tiny colored dots of light. From a distance, these dots merge together to make a multicolored picture, and we are not aware of the dots. A television picture is made up of red, blue, and green dots because these are the primary colors of light. They are different from the primary colors of paint (see page 10).

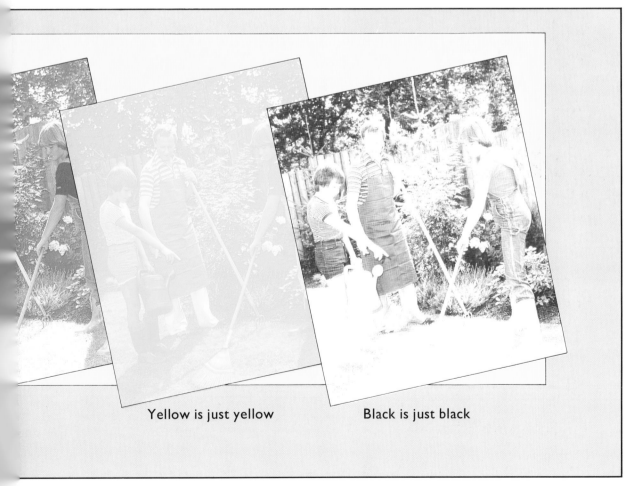

Yellow is just yellow   Black is just black

▲ Have you ever seen a rainbow on a sunny day when it is raining? Rainbows sometimes appear in the spray of water from a waterfall too. The raindrops or water drops make the light spread out so we can see the different colors. Some people think they can see the seven different colors in a rainbow—red, orange, yellow, green, blue, indigo, and violet. How many colors can you see in a rainbow?

RAINBOW COLORS

Where have you seen rainbow colors? Take a bowl of water out into some bright sunshine. Put a few drops of motor oil or household oil on the surface of the water. How many colors can you see? What happens if you add more water or more oil? If you stir the water with a stick, do the colors change?

Soap bubbles also have rainbow colors in them. Do big bubbles have different color patterns from small bubbles? Do the colors in a bubble change in sunlight?

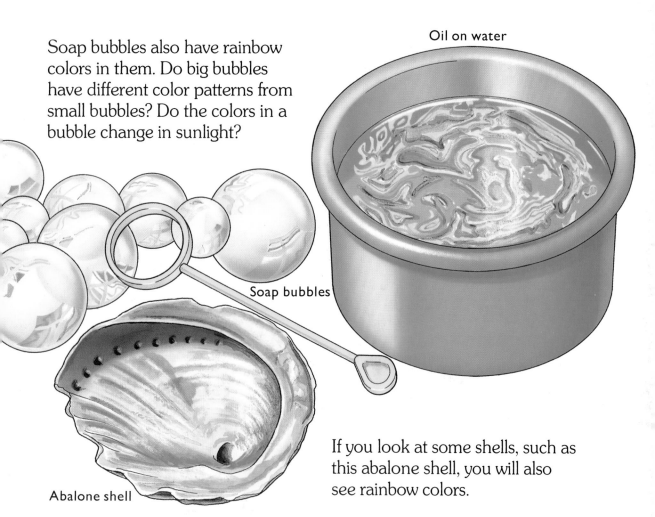

Oil on water

Soap bubbles

Abalone shell

If you look at some shells, such as this abalone shell, you will also see rainbow colors.

The colors in oil, soap bubbles, and some shells are caused by the way light is reflected between the thin outer layers of each object. The rainbow colors are not spread out as they are in a real rainbow.

Prism Rainbow

A specially shaped piece of glass called a prism will spread out the colors in white light to make rainbow colors. This was first seen by the scientist Isaac Newton while he was carrying out some experiments in 1665.

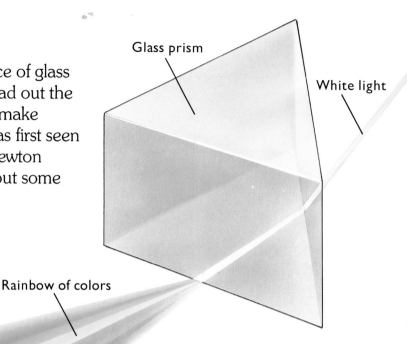

Glass prism

White light

Rainbow of colors

Make a Rainbow

You can make your own prism with a container of water and a mirror. Fill the container with water and hold the mirror at an angle so that sunlight or electric light falls on the mirror. The water in front of the mirror works like a prism, making the light bend. The different colors in the light bend in different amounts so the colors separate. The mirror reflects the rainbow onto a piece of white cardboard or paper, or a wall or ceiling.

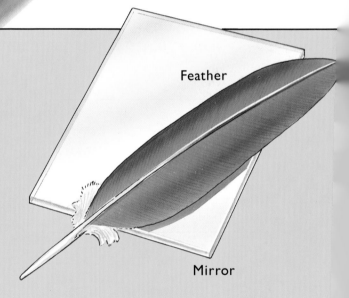

Feather

Mirror

Feather Rainbow

Ask an adult to light a candle for you. Stand about a foot away from the candle and look through a feather's outer edge. As you look through the narrow slits, you will see tiny flames with rainbow colors.

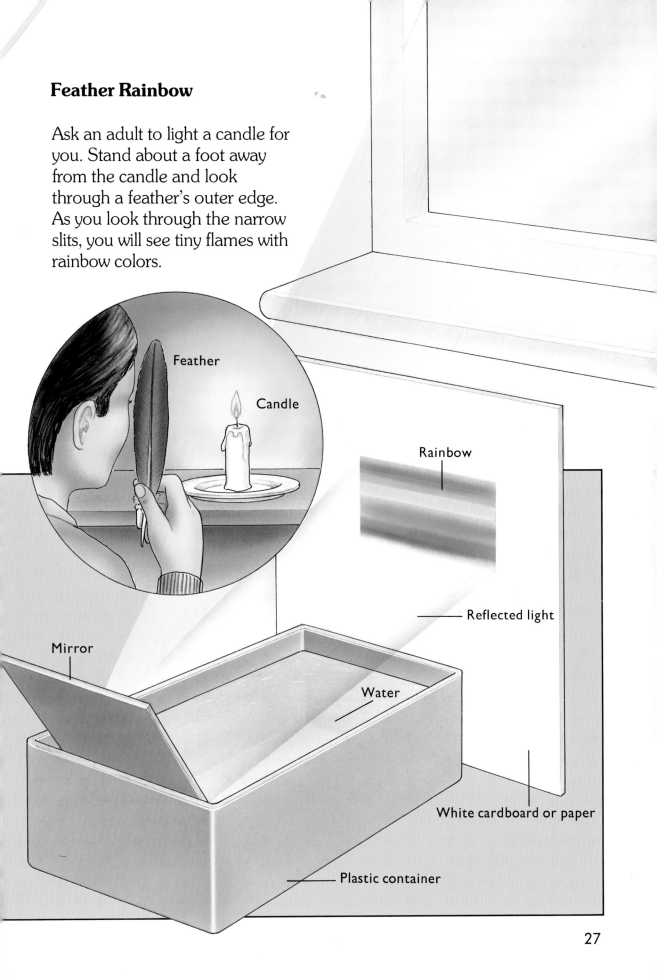

Feather

Candle

Rainbow

Reflected light

Mirror

Water

White cardboard or paper

Plastic container

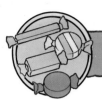

SEE-THROUGH COLORS

Some colored materials, such as glass, Plexiglas, and water, will let light pass through them. They are said to be transparent. If you look through these transparent materials, they change the colors of the things you see.

Make a collection of transparent materials, such as colored bottles, candy wrappings, and plastic. You could also color the water in a clear bottle with ink or food coloring. How do these materials change the color of things you see through them? Is there any difference if you overlap two colors?

What happens

The transparent materials are all types of filters. They let light of the same color pass through, but they stop other colors from getting through. For instance, a red filter lets red light through, but stops the other colors.

▲ If you look at the light coming through a stained glass window, it will be the same colors as the glass itself. Each piece of glass only lets through light of the same color as itself.

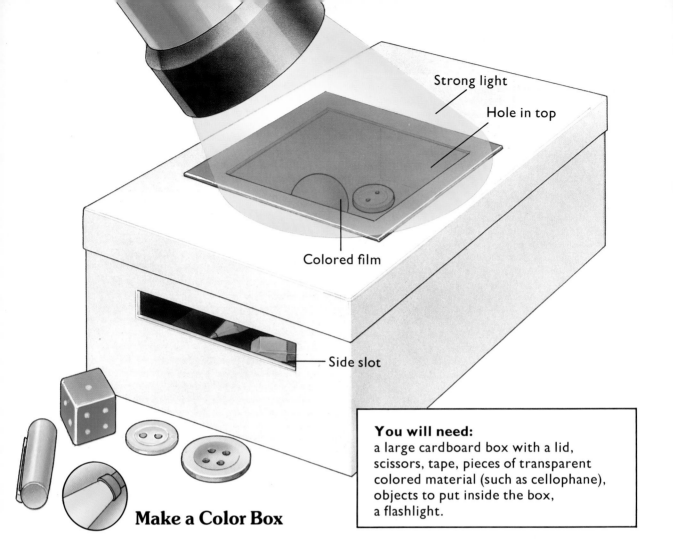

Strong light

Hole in top

Colored film

Side slot

Make a Color Box

You will need:
a large cardboard box with a lid,
scissors, tape, pieces of transparent
colored material (such as cellophane),
objects to put inside the box,
a flashlight.

1. Collect some small objects; be sure to collect at least one object in each color of the rainbow.

2. With an adult's help, cut a large square hole in the lid of the box.

3. Cut a thin, narrow slot in one side of the box.

4. Cut a square of each color of transparent material. Make each square a little bit bigger than the hole in the top of the box.

5. Put the objects in the box.

6. Lay one of the pieces of transparent material over the hole in the top of the box and ask a friend to shine a light down through the transparent material.

7. When you look through the slot in the side of the box, what color do the objects appear to be? Repeat the same test with the other transparent materials and record your results. Can you explain your results? (Hint: Look back at filters on page 28.)

Make Some Color Glasses

You will need:

stiff cardboard, scissors, tape, small pieces of red and green cellophane, a pencil.

1. Draw an outline of the glasses on the cardboard and, with an adult's help, cut out the glasses.
2. Stick red cellophane over one eyehole and green cellophane over the other eyehole.
3. Put on the glasses and see how they change colors around you.

What happens

The red eyepiece lets only red light reach your eye, and the green eyepiece lets only green light reach your eye. So one eye sees only things that reflect red light, and the other eye sees only things that reflect green light.

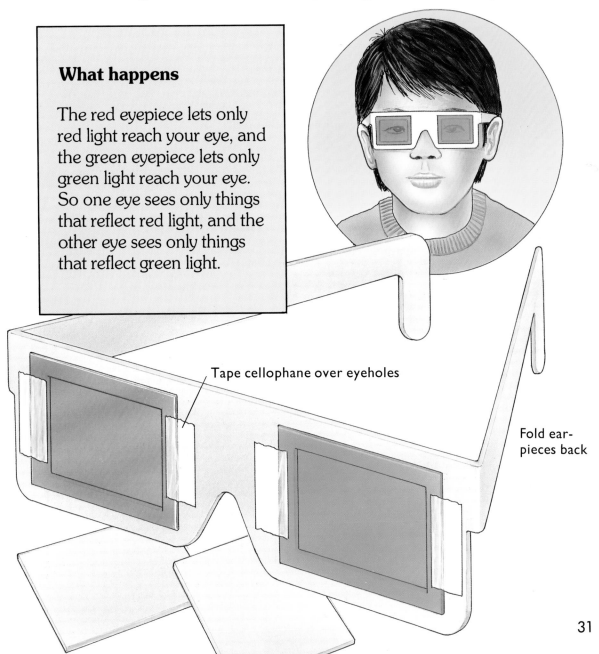

Tape cellophane over eyeholes

Fold ear-pieces back

COLORED LIGHT

Mixing colored light does not give the same results as mixing colored paints. This experiment shows how it is different.

You will need:
three flashlights, pieces of red, blue, and green cellophane, tape, white cardboard.

1. With an adult's help, cut pieces of cellophane that are the right size to fit over the front of the flashlights. Make one flashlight red, one blue, and one green.
2. In a darkened room, shine the red and green flashlights onto the white cardboard. Where the beams of light meet on the cardboard, you should see yellow light.
3. Try mixing blue and green light or blue and red light. What colors do they make?
4. Now try mixing all three colors. What happens this time?

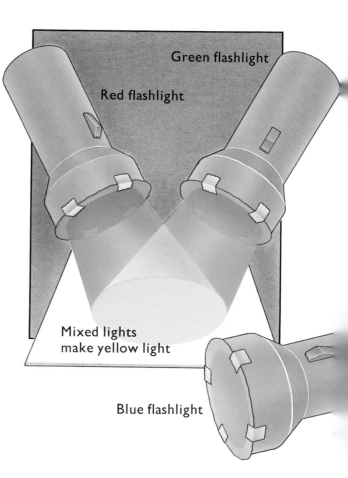

Green flashlight

Red flashlight

Mixed lights make yellow light

Blue flashlight

What happens
All the colors of the rainbow can be made by mixing the primary colors of light, which are red, blue, and green. Can you remember the primary colors of paint? The colors that are made by mixing the primary colors of either light or paint are called secondary colors. Yellow is one secondary color of light. The others are dark pink (magenta) and green-blue (cyan). By mixing all three primary colors of light, you make white light.

▲ Colored lights are often mixed together in different ways to change the atmosphere and create special effects at concerts. Color filters are put in front of white spotlights to light up the stage and make the different colors.

Make a Color Changer

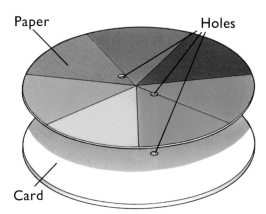

1. With an adult's help, cut out a cardboard circle about 4 inches across.
2. Cut out a circle from white paper the same size as the cardboard.
3. Color the paper circle with the same colors as the picture.
4. Glue the paper circle onto the cardboard.
5. Use a sharp pencil to make two holes as shown.
6. Cut off about a yard of string.
7. Push the string through the holes as shown, and tie the ends together.
8. To spin your color changer, move the circle to the middle of the string. Twirl it around several times to twist the string. Then pull the string very tight so the circle unwinds. As it unwinds, relax the string and the circle will wind itself up again.

What happens
The color changer makes the colors go by so fast that your eye can't see each one separately. Your brain combines some of the colors to make new ones. For instance, your brain turns flashes of blue and red into purple.

Paper   Holes

Card

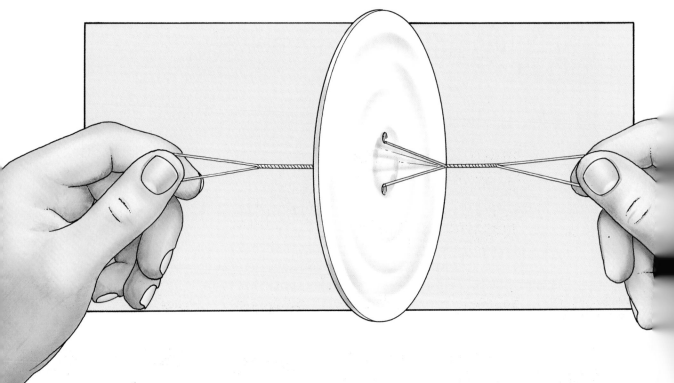

Spinning Colors

Another way to make colored light mix by movement is to make spinning tops. Cut some cardboard circles and color each one in a different mixture of colors. Put a sharp pencil through the middle of each circle and twirl the pencil to make the tops spin. What happens to the colors?

If you make a spinning top with all the colors of the rainbow, it will look white or yellowish when you spin it. All the rainbow colors combine to make white light again.

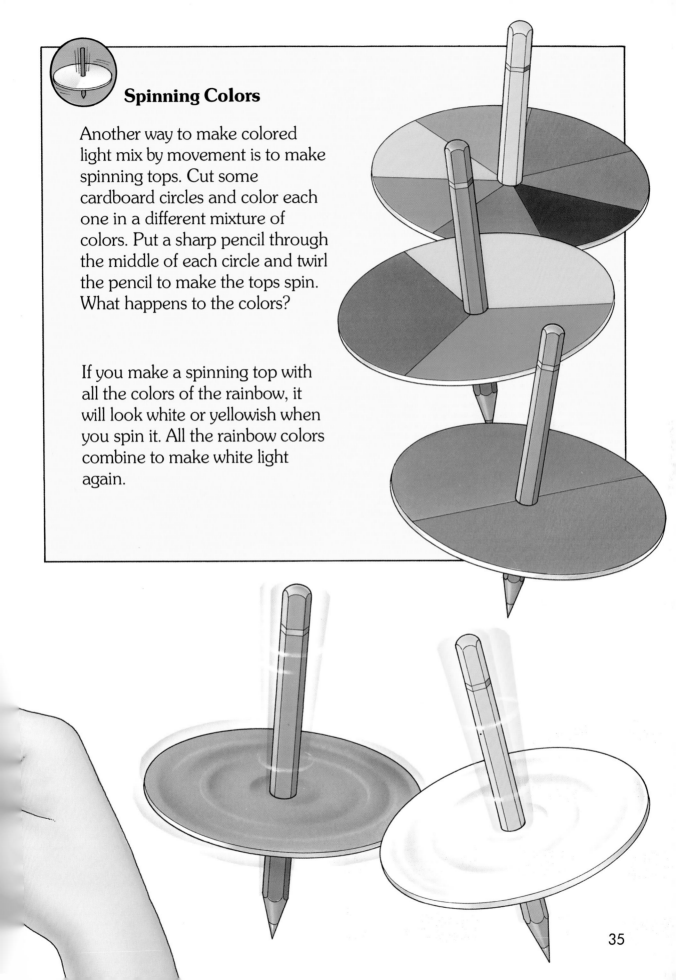

Sky Colors

Have you ever wondered why the sky often appears blue by day and red, pink, or orange at sunrise or sunset? This investigation will show you why this happens.

Fill a tall, clear container with water and put about half a teaspoon of nondairy creamer into the water. Don't stir the water. If you shine a flashlight onto the water from above, it will look a bluish-gray color. Now shine a flashlight through the container from behind. You will find that the water looks an orange-pink color. Try keeping a record of sky colors. What changes occur during a day or a week?

What happens

The earth is wrapped in a blanket of invisible gases called the atmosphere. The atmosphere contains billions and billions of particles that are too small to see. When sunlight hits these particles, the light bounces off them and scatters. Blue and violet light scatter the most; orange and red light scatter the least.

When the sun is low in the sky, at sunrise and sunset, its rays travel through a thicker layer of atmosphere than at midday. Most of the blue is scattered out of the light and only red and orange light are left to color the sky. The same thing happens when you hold the flashlight behind the glass. At midday, the sun is high in the sky, so less light is scattered and more blue light reaches your eyes. This is why the liquid looks blue when you hold the flashlight above the glass.

Volcano Colors

After a volcanic eruption on earth, there are lots of fine particles floating in the atmosphere. Winds carry these particles around the world. The dust particles scatter the blue light, allowing only orange-red light to reach the earth. That is why there are often spectacular sunsets after a big volcanic eruption.

▼ The planet Jupiter is made up mostly of whirling clouds of hydrogen. Other substances are mixed in with the hydrogen and form dark or colored bands. Close-up photographs show red, green, and blue colors in these clouds, which are always changing. The Great Red Spot on Jupiter is a gigantic cloud that is larger than the earth.

ANIMAL COLORS

The colors of animals help them to survive in many different ways. Colors help animals to hide and to attract a mate. Some animals can even change color if their surroundings change.

 Warning Colors

Some animals are poisonous or have a nasty sting. These animals are often brightly colored to warn other animals to leave them alone.

Monarch butterfly caterpillars pick up their poisons by eating the leaves of the milkweed plants. These poisons are passed on to the adults when the caterpillars change into butterflies. Many stinging insects, such as wasps and bees, have black and yellow warning colors.

Colorful Males

Male birds of paradise have colorful, spectacular feathers which they show off in a special display to attract a mate. Sometimes they even hang upside down from the tree branches and wave their feathers up and down. The female birds have fairly plain colors, which helps to hide them from enemies when they are sitting on the eggs.

▲ Chameleons can change their colors by changing the size of spots of pigments in the skin. Their colors often match the colors of the trees and bushes they live in, which helps to camouflage them.

Winter Colors

Some animals, such as the snow-shoe hare, live in places where it snows in winter. They grow a white winter coat that helps them to blend into a snowy background. In spring, they grow a darker colored coat again.

INDEX

Page numbers in *italics* refer to illustrations or where illustrations and text occur on the same page.

Adviser: Robert Pressling
Designer: Ben White
Editor: Catherine Bradley
Picture Research: Elaine Willis

The publishers wish to thank the following for kindly supplying photographs for this book: Page 5 ZEFA; 12 ZEFA; 14 French Government Tourist Office; 16 J. Allan Cash Photo Library; 17 Dylon; 22 The Guardian (top), ZEFA (bottom); 24 ZEFA: 29 ZEFA; 33 ZEFA; 37 NASA; 39 Biofotos.

First Random House edition, 1992

Library of Congress Cataloging-in-Publication Data

Taylor, Barbara, 1954–
  [Color and light (Warwick Press)]
  Over the rainbow!: the science of color and light/Barbara Taylor.—1st Random House ed.
  p.—cm.—(Step into science)
  Reprint. Originally published: Color and light. New York: Warwick Press, 1991. Originally published in series: Fun with simple science.
  Includes index.
  Summary: An introduction to the science of color and light using simple science experiments to show how people and animals see colors, how to make colors, and how to use them in painting, printing, and other projects.
  ISBN: 0-679-82041-8 (pbk.)
  1. Color—Juvenile literature. 2. Color—Experiments——Juvenile literature. 3. Colors—Juvenile literature. 4. Light—Juvenile literature. 5. Light—Experiments—Juvenile literature. [1. Color—Experiments. 2. Light—Experiment. 3. Experiments.] I. Title. II. Series: Taylor, Barbara, 1954– Step into science.
  QC495.5.T4   1992
  535.6—dc20   91-4291

Manufactured in Hong Kong 10 9 8 7 6 5 4 3 2 1